Poems for Friends

– RUTH INGRAM –

Printed and bound in England by www.printondemand-worldwide.com

http://www.fast-print.net/bookshop

Poems for Friends
Copyright © Ruth Ingram 2018
Cover Photo - Ruth Ingram

ISBN: 978-178456-578-7

First published 2018 by
FASTPRINT PUBLISHING
Peterborough, England.

A Burial of words

Unfortunately my poetry is
impuissant to move a publisher.

All seem to think it illaudable;
the last poem illapsing an insignificant
infuscating and only worthy to inhume
as should all words of the ingram.

impuissant   *powerless*
illaudable   *not worthy of praise*
illapsing   *to slide or glide into*
infuscating   *clouded with brown*
inhume   *bury in the earth*
ingram   *ignorant*

Approaching ninety

Seven o'clock
and in the half-dark
the room breathes
memories.
The empty chairs
invite past lives.

Do I have a passport
to an easy death?
I look for it
in all the drawers
of my mind.
It will come soon.

What will remain of me?
A little dust,
a fleeting memory
and perhaps
some fertile earth.

School 1936

School was where you got punished.
Where you were stupid, and sat with the
suffering, silent dunce of the class.

You might be a Jew, so your head
was measured, and so you knew for sure
you were taught that mother could be wrong

if she didn't agree with what the great
Führer wanted, for he obeyed
God, and so was always right.

You hurried home after school, so the boys
could not get hold of your plaits
to drag you painfully along.

It was nice to have a temperature
a respectable high one at that
which made you shiver and burn

safe in bed, where you were tended
with caring hands, and later treated to
wonderful fruit and ice cream.

The temperature only went down
a little over the weeks, and you
noticed went up if you read a lot.

A very enjoyable time;
fruit, ice cream, a safe warm bed
and lots of lovely books.

A doctor was called after three weeks.
He found no disease. Mother lost patience
You had to get up *with* a temperature.

And back to school.

Letter to my Body 2015

You've failed me again!
You say
you are me
but
you are my servant.

I
want to walk in the autumn sun
but my eyes
can't see the pavement
and my legs sway uncertainly
threatening to fall.

I
looked after you
for so many years
fed and watered your multitude
of demanding cells.

How ungrateful you are!

I
walked along rivers
across fields and woods
and all over town.
Now you leave me , when I most need you
just to go down the street.

How inconsiderate of you!

You say I am worn out
like my threadbare carpet
and need replacing
I don't agree –
at any rate
not just yet.

So when you finally leave me
will you take me with you?

To my body 2017

I feed you and give you to drink
you ungrateful old thing!
Anyone could think
I didn't look after you –
you know that's not true!

Your legs flail about without direction
don't do as their told, won't go upstairs
and give themselves airs,
think others should do so
while they stay below.

No shopping, no cooking, and No
washing up: What's got into you?
Now you refuse to go?
Won't even make the attempt
Believe your exempt.

And now you've a cancer
on top of your head
What's it doing there?
Cover it up, put it to bed!

You've got no control: –
One eye has gone awol
Give it direction!
Don't allow such defection!

You failed me again! You say you are me
but you are my servant, you have to agree.

Your memory is going
and my memory has gone
She slipped through a keyhole
and left me alone.

So you don't know any names
and I hardly my own.

Tree of Life

My home was in you
and the mighty chestnut tree
outside our window, blest us both.

Now I sleep in my single bed
my tree of life cut down
the site developed into indifferent stone.

Quite soon your life ended too
in an alien hospice bed – but there
a nurse entered, known from

another life. *They know me here*
you said, a time from when
you were at home in your profession

not divested of your skills, your status
the respect which had been given you
long in the past replaced

by a condescending pity.
They know me here you said
at home with yourself again -
you died.

St. John's Cave

They streamed like ants towards the shrine
driven by their certain belief in his power
to heal all their pain and suffering in this life.

I joined them
not sharing their faith.

As I approached the cave, all fell silent.
In the dim interior candles flickered in a recess
and opened up a great spirit
of holiness – unforeseen.

And like all the pilgrims I lit a candle
for you.

I am old

but the sun rises
in me
this bright day.
The wind springs to life
my winter limbs
wakes up my youth
opens my eyes to
the brilliance of a geranium
the greening of trees
and the little coal tit
pecking an ivy leaf.

In a Romanian Hospice

You lie on your little thin arm
a dank wisp of hair on your forehead
dark eyes turned inwards
waiting to die.

What mother abandoned you?
Was she too sick to care and
where was your father?

Ten years old.
Too young to know the beauty
of your arched eyebrows,
and long elegant hands.

Would you have been a musician,
or a sculptor?

Why did your life begin
to end like this?

Refugee

'I write in English but my memory of those damp autumn leaves is in
Bulgarian. This is why I could only be a tenant in the English language
house.'   *(Kapka Kabanova)*

Losing a home
losing a language
in which to live,
to see, to feel, to touch
to be a person:
heat glancing off cobbles,
wind in the cherry blossom
frost-bitten winter hands
comfort of featherbeds
all took root in us
and grew into language.

We came to strange sounds
and a stranger way of being
we adapted, diminishing
ourselves,
learned to be other
than we are.

Now we are legion,
those of us who survive.
We the remnants
have no past to cherish
no future to hope
a present which is fear
where we have become
alien to ourselves.

Boys

1.
My parents taken
I escaped
My yellow star
hidden.

I found a cellar
seen from my window

and waited –

and waited –

What for?

Till they
come
for me.

2.
They took me
when I was ten
taught me to kill
for Allah.

Sent me
to target
the enemy

who hunts me
at every border
in every country.

I was promised
martyrdom
so I walk –

and walk –

towards
death.

A London Death 2017 (Inspired by M. Kaléko)

A Polish builder dies. His wife stares into empty days –
the loss of life she knew too great for tears.

His foreman sends condolences, his English mates
who generally despised him say: 'He will be missed'.
But since he's dead it doesn't matter much.

The local paper states: 'Builder killed at work'.
So, with his zero hours contract, his wages
and her income cease immediately.

The money couldn't cover the expense,
although the undertaker made a small reduction.
His relatives who never liked her, now contest his will.

To her, who loved him, it seems the world has stopped.
But all that's changed is that there's far less money
and friends tend to avoid her now.

New Year Ditty 2018

The old year died, there's a dark decline –
targets we had didn't happen as yet: –
for changing the climate
and bombing for peace
and giving new life
to rhinos
and tigers
by killing the beasts.

There have been
meetings
and treaties
promises and threats
likely scenarios
and unlikely bets
that all will be well
with a stock market boom
and great manufacture
to export and consume
as for the wars far from our shore –
as they get nearer
we can bomb them
some more.

On my balcony

Tiny green beetle
lost in the hot concrete
desert we made you
seeking shelter from
the burning sun.

Your demented search
for your lost world
continues up the mountain
of a black plastic pot
the utopia of flowers
far out of reach.

It mirrors our own loss
and that of all the creatures
we have destroyed.

Politician

I am mighty –
a mountain among men.
On the south side
I am peaceful, sun-blest,
with gentle slopes
inviting crowds
to my native flora and fauna.

But try me from the east –
there alien foreigners
will need crampons and rope
to scale my defences
and their assault will
rouse my sleeping fires
to rise from my bowels
to shatter their illusions
and spew them out
into their face.

On this spring morning

a street is demolished.
A six-year old
sits on the little stool
his father made
he glares defiantly
at the soldier
and refuses to move –
his sisters have long
left weeping.

On this spring morning
A young girl lies alone
bleeding in the dust
the acrid smoke of her
burnt village
in her nostrils.

But now
a warm spring wind
sweeps through my hair
young leaves light up
on the old oak tree
and the sun pours
over my winter-weary limbs
on this spring morning.

**Questions
or 21st century**

Now all certainties have become questions.
Estranged from the computerised world
I look back at the comfort of human connections,
to the sanity of simple living; away
from the glitz and glamour, skating
on thin ice over the destruction
of this, our planet;
helping the fraudulent and brutal to prosper.
The powerful claiming 'justice' for revenge
and their drive to kill.

Others, who have no voice are feared by the rich
as they flee from war, torture and annihilation.

But in this horror, Ali, Street Musician of Damascus
still plays, and children still dance to his music,
and Jenny, nurse from Ireland still tends
the wounded,
though her hospital has been destroyed, and her life
is in danger.

And what are my concerns? One of the few comfortable
in the West?
Stains on my carpet, the latest fashion, or
a third world war?

Eruption

He suffered from an enlarged sense of superiority
It showed up in minor symptoms at first:
a demand for sole attention,
a correction for all who spoke.

What I said seemed to fall beside his chair,
and there was no way I could pick up
the discarded words.

So I went on talking
to fill the empty spaces
between us, like black holes
powered with the gravity
of the unsaid.

But then he provided the grit in my oyster
it chafes at my sides and grows in my eyes,
is filed into fine anger
is sharpened by friction
large and glowing rises in me
until, it bursts out of my mouth.

Ode to my House

You have grown old with me,
and begin to creak at the joints – just like me.

Will you take a stair lift? I'm having trouble
getting to your top.

I see your dry skin flaking off outside
and your soft furnishings wearing thin like mine

I lose words in my head and things inside you;
like keys, my purse, and cooking utensils.

I want to stay in you despite our joint
shortcomings, you are my past my home and my history.

Neither of us were made for the fast
glitzy digital minds of to-day, only

for the slow, enclosed world
where disasters are local

like the stains on the carpet
and the red spots on my face.

I'd like us both to keep up appearances
until I finally have to leave you to someone else.

Night Visitor

Everyone else was out on the tiles
and someone had left a window open

So there he was unlike a real robber
comes to mind

large as life
and three times as natural

about to step into my room
through the open window

Grinning like a Cheshire cat
as though he were

supposed to be there
at eleven o'clock at night

He looked hurt
when I shut him out of my life

When later I described him
to the policeman

as Irish looking with a soft look
and probably professional

The politically correct policeman
said: That's racist!

Haiku

Restless night waiting on sleep
crafting images of catastrophes
into a grey dawn.

Underground rush hour. The train
roars in, disgorges a thousand
anxious city workers.

Sharp in-take of breath
Woodsmoke in clear air. Winter sun
grasses singing frost.

Ode to my little Portuguese

My dear unpretentious little thing
born to be useful in an alley of Lisbon
sold for a few coins alongside a humble
spoon and fork in the Saturday market

you served me for so many years
the sharpest of tools to cut, scrape
and spread; uncomplaining whatever the task.
I miss your talents!

I made cheese on toast, vegetable stews
and apple crumbles for my guests with your
help – I took you for granted. I can reach
the rack full of fancy knives with whorled

and serrated blades, useless for cutting bread,
scraping carrots or spreading butter –
And now you are gone! Where have you
hidden? Were you stolen? Please come back.

Security

Iron railings
a man-made prison
for fuchsias
dying a slow, sad death.

No leaves
on the railway line
so stately maples
hacked
into grotesques.

The parking lot kept
clear
no blade of grass
tolerated.

Spring

and soft winds touch
me,
wake up my
green shoots
to stretch skywards
with young leaves,
open my eyes
to the brilliance
of a geranium
and the little
coal tit
pecking at
an ivy leaf.

Devotion

My ninety year old mother
liked to teach wisdom –
her wisdom, of 'body awareness'
gathered over the decades.

Her principal grief was that
her children would not pay attention,
would not recognize the great gifts
she so willingly gave to all.

So she was delighted, when Isabel,
a young American moved into her flat
to be taught; how to be, to sit, to listen;
something she had apparently

not done in her home state of Idaho.
Isabel explained to me that she had found
her guru. I noticed she had also found
accommodation and good food.

Isabel made up for all my deficits:
told me to kiss my mother more
and find her a good home;
though eventually Isabel's

affectionate advances were not accepted,
my mother told her 'that she was not
the kissing type', and no alternative home
that pleased my mother was found.

Whereupon Isabel left with a promise
to return. Two years later my mother died
and Isabel returned to take up
residence in the flat, and made it

into a shrine; using her inimitable taste;
blue plastic flowers, incense,
and images of herself and her guru.
It took all my mother's ungrateful children

to turn out her devoted student, who had
learned to sit, to listen, and pay attention.

Homo Sapiens

Stardust
blown by solar winds
Homo Sapiens
twenty first century
in their time
without time.

Curious creatures
bent on self-
destruction
residing on a
speck of flotsam
in the cosmos

on the edge
of extinction
spinning myths
to escape
a beautiful world
they destroyed
to a dead planet.

Spring wind

Spring wind lifts
My wings high
With the bird song

I skim over meadows
Alight with celandine
Cowslip and buttercup

Drunk with the sun
And scent of hawthorn
Blossom I fling myself

Into the wind-torn clouds
And my voice
Resounds through the skies.

Locked in the institution of old age

regulated by social distinction
on a restricted diet of

arthritis and
polite condescension
released by
a stranger's sudden smile
the child has escaped

through bars
into the garden of the young
desiring the delights and the life
that has long been withheld.

But the jailor knows
that these luscious fruits
are not to eat –
only the stale parts
of yesterday's rations.

So the child returns behind bars
small and stunted
in an old body.

Winter Gale

A grey, quiet day
low light
only the scrunch of steps
on pebble sand
and sound of lazy, lapping tide.
I trudge along the shore:
no-one in sight.

A light wind stirs
and lifts the calm
brings small drops of rain.
The half-light darkens –
and the wind begins to sing
lifts his voice to whistle
moan and howl
whips rain and sand into my face
twists and bends the trees
hurls rocks and water-spray from hilltops
into a thunderous crashing symphony
sweeps me up into his wild dance.

Listening to Johann Sebastian

I enter cathedrals
of sound reaching
to the rafters up
to the opening skies

Whirling winds of scales
descend in half-tones
to the depths of human
frailty and grief

My sadness expands
across the pews
thoughts of mortality
deepen darker
into the night

To rise again
to the light
and new life

Rapid rivers of music
run in me rushing
down stream into
whirlpools of living waters

Gradually in calmer
pools there is a reverence
a contemplation
of the eternal spirit

Singing the magnificent
songs of his faith
within the tragedies
of man I hear
the single small notes
in their isolation

reaching the contradictions
of the mighty fugue
the voices intertwine
and resolve into
exquisite melody

From the Tory Hymnal

It's a necessity
to grow the economy
without opposition
so we have the condition
under strong stable government
to cut public services
It makes for certainty
in times of austerity.

There is no need for reduction
in corporate taxation
for shares to increase
and so to release
the potential
of business and
executive pay.

Most needs can be met
by volunteers
for the deserving
homeless and blameless
so we'll do charity
instead.

It's good for
our image
avoids the fraudsters,
illegals
and beggars
brings votes
to the party
and electoral success.

Pub lunch

London garbage invades my head
Musack, beer cans, broken glass. So
I've lost the few thoughts I've ever had.

I strain hard to catch what has been said
It's usual before replying to know.
London garbage invades my head.

It's supposed to be social this breaking of bread
You shout and scream in constant flow
I've lost the few thoughts I've ever had.

In spite of the speaker blasts overhead,
We still continue this ridiculous show
London garbage invades my head.

I try to make sense of what has been said
But I can't put together words that I know
I've lost the few thoughts I ever had.

Perhaps just now I'm going stark mad
Exhaustion makes me painfully slow
London garbage invades my head
I've lost the few thoughts I ever had.

City bird

Here on the roof
in the city
surrounded by
the ebb and flow
of traffic
like a sea -
soft winds
on my face
and the first sun
to lift my spirit.
Voices rise from below
shouting, laughing
and above
on the next roof
a blackbird
announces
his spring.

City night

Night voices
pulsing through
hot thick darkness.
Undercover laughter,
and whisper,
and stifled cry.

Lone panic of
enclosing walls'
ear-splitting silence
endured
till first light.

and somewhere
disco rock
filling vast hunger
with decibels
to shake the streets
and drown fear
in oblivion.

Menace
of distant police sirens
becoming insistent
nearing, swelling
into a scream.

Good intentions

I found her early, before I knew her name
She grew into a graceful plant in March
with glossy leaves and tender upright stem.
Her buds began to swell in early May
and one June morning burst into a fan
of delicate lemon bloom.
Her rich scent filled my room.

I fed her, I watered her, and put her in the sun;
but slowly she turned against the sky
and dropped her flowers, one by one.
I saw her droop, and thought I heard her sigh.

I bought her remedies of every kind
and sought professional aid, but still
she languished, and looked as though she'd die.

At last I thought she was too sick to live
so I broke her stem and pulled her by the roots
to end the suffering, but then I saw
what I had done: her sap was rising still -
she was not dead, but I had killed her then.

Morning Fox

He stood on the wall
Behind the house
In his shining coat
Curious to
Smell the new day

Stared me out
Unflinching –
Boldly held me in his eye
to tell me: 'You
haven't destroyed me
yet.'

I came here in the empty dark

I came here in the empty dark
far east of the known city
into alien streets.
No connections: no train, no bus;
only menacing houses
with dead eyes.

I was to be met at the last 'phone box
but no-one rang and no-one came.
If I wait here longer
there will be no chance
of a known road.

All my life I have spun thin threads
to connect, to send a message -
but most tore in the wind and noise
of world traffic.
Now it was the last.

Daffodils

As I was walking
down the street
I thought I saw
my neighbour's curtain
which had been drawn
all the week, pulling
slowly back, or
at any rate moving to
the extent of showing
a small vase on the window-sill
in which she always kept
one or two dead daffodils
to remind her of her
husband's death
since he had been
particularly fond of
these renaissance flowers
that is to say
the pale yellow ones
which matched
his complexion
and which for this
reason she preferred
to keep in the house
as some sort of sign
of his continued presence
in her life.

Underground Shelter Grozny 2000

This night started long before dusk,
this cellar -time was there without memory
of sky, or street, or any living thing
above ground.
Only coughing and vomit
and human stench in the darkness.

A hundred eyes still questioning , hoping,
expectant of the morning
and the possible escape routes:
to the country
to Ingushetia
to the sea -
Still dividing
the rice, the water, the mouldering bread
into portions
to last a day? a week? a month?

So the night spun out, hour after tense hour
and still the hair-thin hope
that some day, some time this would end.

But then it came
with a roar from above
a rending, a tearing, a fury of fire
Afterwards - silence
and a fine dust rising.

Kings Cross

Ten summers and ten winters long
she lives alone, abandoned on the street
even the memory of her mother gone.
At night she lies on rags, a dirty sheet
to keep her warm. Today a woman
she looks for easy warmth, however fleeting
from passing strangers young and old - a man
who will respond to her insistent pleading.
And I, who never knew her life, assuming
that she's insolent in her urgent importuning
have turned away from her distress, and do not meet
her vacant stare, nor recognize the child in her
so that her dreary world does not impinge on me
a world which no-one wants to see.

Leaves

They fell in twisted shapes , casting long shadows
in the November sun.
each one a history of summer

The pavement glistens
from last night's rain to make a precious
grave of polished stone.
they glow in red-green gold
 - their final glory. Then turning brown
and dying. Withered, swept away – like us discarded.

Heat-wave over stubble fields

Wide meadows
Limitless skies

Immensity

Midday stillness

And in the waiting silence
A lark's voice rising
From horizon to horizon

opening the skies.

It happened

After the dance
time halted
held me suspended
the night became alive
it began to breathe in me
its clear frosty breath
opened the gates
and I entered
becoming sky
and moonlight
and immensity.

Young

Alone
here on windswept
Zeeland
filled with March sun
the glinting grass
bends double.

I spread my sails
and travel
far out to sea –
leave my body
as the wind
takes me
into sky.

To a paralysed friend

That night you cried for the never-again experience
of the wind on the hills you could not reach
and the high views of fields, with the tree line
stretching into the haze of earth-ending sky.

In the morning, after the rain, the sky cleared
Each leaf trembling in the young light
And you looked up, and you laughed in new delight.

St. Agnes Scilly Isles

Time expands over the islands with early light
whitening sea-spume
lifting shadows from far rocks
and all life lived before mine.

A flock of terns fly up into the clearing sky
Nearer, where the tide is out
a subdued whistling, and clacking of beaks
early morning gossip of

greenshank, oystercatcher and turnstone
as they scuttle and run between rocks and
seaweed, feeding from glistening sand.

And as the sun touches the shore
the last mists rise, revealing
this day in my life.

In a village churchyard.

Midsummer stillness.
only the whirr of damselfly wings.
Scent of fresh grass
and meadow-sweet
growing between glittering flint-stones
in the ruined church
abandoned for a century.
Brambles cover the gravestones
I sit to read one inscription:

'Edith Burrill spinster of this parish
Died 1840 aged twenty years'.

She came here exhausted from the fields
to be alone and pray
for the life in her to come.
sitting on a stone,
the sun hot on her back,
as it is on mine .

He had promised to marry her.
Now she would hold her own
with the married women,
no longer afraid of gossip.

Wild grasses blow over the grave.

A poem

A poem is like
a blown grass seed
that flies lightly
and settles not in any
explicable manner

germinates, in the unknown
unaware, innocently;
lives incognito.

Perhaps harbours
minute life forms
which may grow
into shimmering
winged beetles

or merely larvae,
which don't survive.

Just occasionally
the shoot provides
a supple post
for a spider to spin
a temporary home

until the blade
now grown long and thin
turns dry and brittle,
dies unnoticed
wondering whether
it was a poem.

Arrest

No-one will hear, no-one will know
how he was taken. The only witness
black glistening pavement and
soft falling rain.

His breath stopped
ice seeped through his veins.
He heard high violins
drawing him in to unearthly worlds
in a shimmer of pain.

I saw you last night

I was sitting on the old bench
looking out on the ivy-covered shed
soft Cornish rain dripping
on the window-sill.

Matthew had come in with
some new-laid eggs
and Sheila was frying a big breakfast.

Familiar and warm, the smell
of fresh toast, bacon and coffee
enveloped me in blissful comfort.

Then I saw you coming down the stairs
touching the banister lightly.

I wanted to say something to you
but I could not reach you -
Your eyes grew frightened at the edges,
as though you knew what was to come;
and you eluded me.

When at last I saw you again
you did not know me
so I called out -
but you were already elsewhere.

I asked Sheila where you had gone
She looked at me coldly and said:
'Where we all go' –

After he died

Re-starting my journey
where the path is unknown
irregular, in sandy soil,
splitting in many ways –
most lost in the sand.

Others have gone this way
before me, but have left
no signpost.

The terrain has changed,
now there is spiky undergrowth
to block every path

each footstep has to be tested.
I need to look for the ants
to trace their way and connect

with what I am searching for –
I need to listen intently
to the sounds previously neglected.

All I can do, is to keep open, alive –
not to give up, learn
to discard the fear of life

allow myself to be driven
past the rocks of the deep swirling
currents, to flow with the great
river towards
the sea.

Grief

She had lived here for so many years –
knew every street, every short cut,
but now he had died she couldn't find
                    her way home;
nothing was familiar, the road seemed
        to move away from her
and the houses began to sway uneasily
                    blocking her path.
Cars sped past while she stood undecided
                        in the road
when she reached the pavement she nearly
                    collided with a scooter.
She continued her search, but it led her
                further into the unknown.

Night passing

Dipping in and out of waves
to feed on old stories below,
water flowing from my long body,
I rise to glimpse a distant horizon in the
still darkening night.
I dive again and find you –
a stranger, but
intimately known
you recede as I come near
and dissolve
in the immensity of ocean.

Faces appear from my yesterdays
intent on their own journeys.
The shifting light wavers
I am seventeen, cold in my thin dress
longing, with the scent of white roses
not daring to hope -
on the edge of a miracle
I drift up
to a cold grey dawn.

For Roderick

The world tides wash over you and
the great seas of time take you
into the depths of memory;
sounds of your voice and smile
receding, becoming harmony
with the many voices gone
before you.

Some mourned,
many forgotten.

The breakers draw further
away from the shore,
faces fading into
a distant twilight.
Visiting now is only
in dreams of the still living
soon to spin out into
the unknowable deep.

Please tell someone

Please tell someone
I'm dead.

I wanted to leave a note
but there was no-one to write it
or make a 'phone call
so instead -
Please tell some one
I'm dead.

There's washing up
in the sink,
the gas bill to pay
the cat to go out
the fridge to turn off
my clothes sent to Oxfam,
my account to be stopped.

Perhaps tell a neighbour
and maybe the post
the friends who have gone
specially the man
who once smiled
long years ago.

My regrets in the dustbin
to be put out at noon
with the rubbish
my remains , and the cat.

Please tell someone
"She's dead".

End of day

Death of a sister

Why was this journey made?
Begun in the morning of another age
a trusting child eager to touch
discover, brimful of laughter.

But soon to retreat,
become discordant
fragmented, alone.

Now, nearing the final destination,
all the fragments lie
on a hospital bed
and we, the unrelated relatives,
sit by her who is not yet dead
attempt to know one another
hour after hour
while the light on the wall fades
the day closes:
There are no last rites
no ceremony for this
long, un-remarked journey.

We who are old

We who are old, we have this present space
free of all hope and needless fear
we know our time is coming near
and all life offers is relentless pace.
We too were children in an unending spring
filled with the promise of a future love.
Later we knew that this was not enough
and took a harder path toward amassing
learning, and goods and recognition
setting our goals with some ambition -
such ways we had to make amends
for loss of life, and love and friends
but now we have this brilliant sky
this tree, this flower, this life before we die.

Looking in the Mirror

Who are you?
Should I have known you old man
when I was ten, racing
to leap across the roof-tops
which none of my friends dared do.

Should I have known you when I was twenty
and stayed up all night dancing, hoping
that she would notice me,
notice that I could throw my partner
into the air, and give her more pleasure
than any man on the dance floor.

Should I have known you as myself
when I climbed the Eiger, and afterwards
entertained a whole crowd?
And later still, when I was what people
call mature (but still with a fine head of hair)
when I was in command of a squadron
and my men listened and respected
everything I said and did; needed my permission.

Should I have known you, given you so much
as a glance? A bald morose old geezer
who can't do the stairs by himself,
who can't remember where he put his spectacles
or his keys - or sometimes exactly where he lives
or whether he saw anyone to-day -

No-one wants to know you now, not if they
can help it, not if they can get away with an excuse.

Monkey Mind

Wait till I catch you!
I know you're there
up in that tree
looking at me.
Now spit out
those chewed
thoughts
and come down
to me.

You leap to next year
and into my past
you know this is useless
and can't possibly last
hang by your tail
to point out attractions
then hand me distractions
like rotten old nuts.

You lose me
confuse me
and leave me behind
when I've made up my mind.

You're up to your tricks
when it comes to decisions
then at once
there are three of you
with your endless chatter
(though none of you matter),
and each time I look
I can't find even one
since none
of you is
ever
quite
There.

Not quite a Terza Rima

Unusual I thought at first glance, but pleasing -
A strange hat, and a talkative man.
Then my faint interest turned towards liking.

Your dress extraordinary, your beard partisan,
unlikely, untried, and quite unforeseen
you looked up astonished , your humour deadpan.

So while I was working my usual routine
I dropped all my plans and ended up laughing
and forgot altogether where I had been.

At last simply rooted and not quite knowing
I listened and followed without interruption
until it grew dark, and all were departing.

So now what you said has become an obsession,
an all-day event and often disturbing.
Significant? or merely what I imagine?

I know I could hug you, but could this be loving?

Junior school teacher required

Bare concrete corridor lead her on her way
pervaded by a smell of gym shoes, and small unwashed boys
a settled gloom lies over dark low-ceiling rooms
filled with worn out, name-scratched desks;
no picture anywhere relieves a wall.

In the assembly hall she's beckoned to approach -
Her inquisition sits beneath a list of gold-emblazoned names;
survivors who attained the fabled grammar school.

They test her faith in rules and rituals of the school's tradition
her willingness to submit to these confining walls of thought
She needs the job; dressed carefully to please -
but now half suffocates in heavy air of stifled life
that ghosts the atmosphere; and when offered the position
'with regret' declines.

Govinda's Gods

Born untouchable
I avoided her
who is high caste.

Her sari blew in the wind
and her slim ankle
caught my eye.

I pray to Krishna
my beautiful blue God
beloved by all

he who can entice
women and plays
divine melodies

I want to live and love
like him and will
worship him

if he will take away
my birth as a Dalet
and give her to me

Or should I worship
Vishnu destroyer and creator
of the world

so that I become all-powerful
destroy all obstacles and
take possession of her?

Yet, I still hunger for a God
who will protect me
from all my desires.

The Lord's Helpers

When it's dark, and lights are out
me and me Dad goes in. there's no doubt
we're first class craftsmen for a start
and we got practice in our Art.

When I legged the wall
I knew there'd be a haul
I'm an expert mechanic, so I picked the door
With a bag on the table I knew there'd be more.

So I helps myself to me just reward
for it's blessed by the Lord
Didn't he say "Give all to the poor?"
and she's got plenty for sure –
But to me she gave nought

so I helps her out,
that's what I done.

Morning contemplations

Flat grey light
Winter dawn.
I am desert-dry.
All living waters damned up
by great boulders

and not the slightest green blade
of an idea in my head.
No-one expecting me;
time to write
think, contemplate
to be.
And all that comes is
a little trickle of
cliché

The ground waters are out of reach
so it's no use scratching in the dry sand.

Yesterday it came to me
that I can receive and adapt
to others' moods and desires
causing the illusion to arise
of understanding, meeting.

It flatters me to be so entrusted:
a comfortable place to be
avoiding conflict
and the full glare of
accurate perception.

Being the recipient
the sound of my voice
hardly emerges clearly
between our two glass walls
there is an illusion of touch -

Only in rare moments
sustained by silence
a meeting, a glimpse of the
great spaces beyond.

The Visit

I'm offered six kinds of biscuit
on her very best china –
to make the visit
worth my while.
She says: "He's had chemo
he won't be joining us."

She shows me with pride
the flowering cyclamen
she has nurtured for me
during the weeks of
my absence.
Thanks me profusely
for coming.

She offers coffee – but
clutching the kettle forgets,
while she pours a torrent of words
a tangled stream
of cousins, uncles and half-brothers

all survivors distributed
over three continents;
darning , weaving pulling together
the holes in her life
losing the thread –
was it the cousin a year younger or older?

I am unable to follow
while she tries to put her shattered life
together for the second time
since she came with the Kindertransport.

Unexpectedly he staggers into the room
Unable to speak, he departs almost at once.

A brilliant sky shines through
the kitchen window as we sit
imprisoned in her incomprehensible story.

What's in a name

Moni [mohni]

The girl who
was happy to be at home
with her brother
going to the South Pole
on their sledge, making igloos
under the table
taking the dolls
on long ice tracks.

Moni
the child who got dressed
under the featherbed
in the dark cold
winter mornings
putting on layers
of vests, petticoats
woollens and thick
stiff boots
to walk
unwillingly to school
just before dawn.

Moni
who sat in the row
for the most stupid
in the class; frightened
unable to do arithmetic
finding everything
difficult, asked
if she was Arian.

Moni
who came home from school
with a high temperature
was put to bed
and looked after
didn't have to go to school
and discovered that
when she read late at night

her temperature went up
and she could stay in bed.
Until her mother got tired
and made her go back to school
with or without
a temperature.

England sounded
like the land of Angels
the ferry, the sea,
the journey –
she was still
Moni

Later at English boarding school
she was no longer Moni
She was Moony or Moan ee
a girl with thin plaits
and an ugly accent
wearing cast-off clothes
which didn't fit –
an unnecessary addition
to any girls' group.
They didn't need
Moan ee.

Years later
she decided
she would no longer
be that person
and chose to use
another name
a freedom she took
from all that
past history.

A love song for Peter Pears

We heard the curlews of oboe and flute
in the wind through the reeds at Snape
and you intoned them in my music.

We walked together at the wild North Sea
your voice towering above the orchestral roar
of incoming tide.

An upbeat, of resounding joy
Then in delicate stepped descent
in my melodies I accompany you until the stream

of lower voices join in a torrent of music
and I become the raging river that carries
you down into the darkness of my demons.

But out of the turmoil, becalmed by violins
your pure high tones rise again,
and my love soars with your voice

to become the centre
of my life.

Peter Pears was the life-long lover of Benjamin Britten
(much of Britten's music was written for Pears)

First Love

Raindrops.
'Stars in your hair'
he said. But I was
already in the galaxy

Invited to eat
I could only see him
and had no need of food.

I thought she was his
and was torn with jealousy
but she didn't want him.

Instead she warned:
'don't let him kiss you'
Then I knew, if he did
I would go up in flames.

In the floods of Time

In the rivers of forgetting
my memory has become islands
leaving remote moments of childhood

held embedded in a long life:-
a cobbled street shaded by huge maples,
the boy running after a horse and cart

to gather horse manure in a dust pan,
the cry of gulls by the river
and the little white boats to take you to town.

But as the flood waters rise
they have submerged much of the past
leaving a morass of uncertain history

of friendships, faces names and places
events remembered in part, the more recent
rapidly forgotten, sometimes submerged.

But sunlit hights endure - the time I came to you
early, you were not expecting me
both of us wordless, amazed and in love.

Cello solo for a post-nuclear age

Comment on a recital without notes

Bow stabs over
sharp craters

Then a low booming
lost in deep caverns

A scraping, a scratching
a sudden screech -
a slide to painful heights

Explosion

Strings still vibrate
burnt in solar rays

Steep descent -

Darkness.

A whisper, a whimper,
dust rising.

The artist on his work

I don't disturb with colour or shape
there are hidden agendas I need to conceal;
you must view from below, and it will reveal
an original idea of the space it might take –
I skate on the edge of fragmented being
hence a specialist method I have of seeing.
It needs constant study to know my intent,
it won't do just to look, and know what is meant.

Turner Prize

I'm named for the Turner Prize
The critics praised me up to the skies
My work is original, dynamic
And totally organic.

An installation
To cover each room
Every day will be new
A totally natural production
In exquisite hue
Of gold and brown
Textured in hard and soft matter
I'll be performing the latter.

And the whole show is enhanced
By including each sense
Thus a strong fragrance
Pervades the whole show
With accompanying sound

You ask how did I do
all that?
Well, I simply shat.

I have left life in the attic

She is not properly insured
and too large
to fit my briefcase.

And anyway, obsolete now
that I can get
'New Sensation'
up on my screen:
it comes in
regular,
intermittent,
and peak.

Moreover, you can buy
a portable attachment
for relationship
(if you go in for
that sort of thing):
straight, gay, parental
or you can play
with all three.

Guaranteed safe,
hygienic and
painless.

If someone later
finds life in the attic
she may still be
of historical interest.

The whole of my Head

The whole of my head is stuffed with waste paper
detritus of adverts; notes of appointments made,
interesting articles , garden advice to look at later.

There are numerous dates and letters mislaid.
No space for thought: just lists of shopping
tax returns, timetables and bills left unpaid.

Programs of concerts that once seemed appealing
brochures of courses never attended
the assault of papers has left me reeling -

I've drafts amended (all judgment suspended)
while sorting and losing and mostly confusing
whatever it was that I should be remembering.

But it goes on with appeals and offers (unwanted),
take- away menus that come through the door
and now here to-day there is more and more and more!

Mato's Lament

Come children all, and hear me speak
a tale of long ago
before my life was bare and bleak
and I was brought so low.

I grew in peace and loveliness
a wondrous verdant show
my head held high with flowers above
and tubers white as snow.

I proudly bore potato names
by which I have been known:
King Edwards, Whites and Reds
and no-one heard me moan.

I gave delight to many a child
and many a man and beast.
My kingdom stretched from furthest west
to Europe and far away East.

I mated with my own dear kind
and all I produced was good.
Nowhere could you my equal find
on farm in field or wood.

But came the day when it was said
potatoes should be square and red
and juicy, clean with softest skin
in perfect shape for boxing in.

A tomato grew in innocence
she had no love for me
I only knew her distantly
but it would seal our destiny

They forced a marriage without consent
I know not why, they did not say,
I know they took my genes away
and left me how I was not meant.

Now no potato can you find.
All that is left is where I rest
in Mato's white and wobbly breast
with a big red bottom behind.

Song of the G8

We wanted dollars
and power
new markets
and oilfields
more cars
and motorways
cheap flights
and hair sprays
and of course
fighter planes.

So we didn't much care
when earth's fragile
dress tore
till she burned
with a roar
and the sun's fire
stripped the forests
the fields
and the life
of the planet
spewing out
corpses human
and animal
crashing the
ice caps
into the oceans
swelling the waters
to swallow the land.

But, we've had
dollars
and flowers
from Israel,
and beans
from Kenya
and wine from Chile
grapes from South Africa
and cars
and motorways
and cheap flights

and holidays
and of course fighter planes
So we don't much care
since we won't be there.

Index	Page